Toy Joy

Written by Dennis McKee

Illustrated by Ellen Sasaki

STECK-VAUGHN
COMPANY

A Division of Harcourt Brace & Company

Joyce owned a big toy shop. She named it
Toy Joy. One day a truck brought some new
toys to Toy Joy.

Joyce opened each box of toys. There were
toys for girls. There were toys for boys. Some
of the toys made noises. Other toys could
hold coins.

3

Joyce found Roy the Cowboy. Roy was
dressed in cowboy clothes. He had a rope
coiled up in his hand. Roy the Cowboy looked
like a friendly toy.

4

Joyce placed the new toys on the shelves.
She put Roy on a shelf, too. Joyce knew boys
and girls would love her new toys. She smiled,
turned off the light, and left to go home.

Roy looked from shelf to shelf. "Maybe one of these toys will be my friend."

"Howdy!" Roy said to Troy the Pig.

Troy turned up his snout and just oinked.

6

Roy walked over to Noisy the Drum.
"Howdy!" Roy said. "Can you play a song?"

Noisy the Drum just sat and sat.

Roy was sad. He had not found any toys
that would be his friends. He sat down on a
shelf. Then he felt a drip, drip, drip. It was oil.

8

"Where's this oil coming from?" asked Roy.

"From me," said Coy the Robot Boy. "I have to oil my joints so that I don't make noise."

 9

"Well, howdy!" said Roy. "I'm a cowboy."

"Howdy back," said Coy. "I'm a robot."

Roy was happy to meet a friendly toy.

"Will you show me around the toy shop?" asked Roy.

"Sure," said Coy. The two toys used Roy's coil of rope to move from shelf to shelf.

Coy showed Roy the toy trucks. "You can ride on them," Coy said. "They also make noises." Roy got on the fire truck.

"These toys can move soil," said Coy. "This one is a dump truck. Hop in."

"Yippee!" said Roy.

"I really enjoy this," said Roy. "Are there any other toys that will join us?"

"Sure," said Coy. "Come on out, all you robot toys!" All the robot toys said howdy.

Click! Slap! Slam!

"Shh!" said Coy. "It's Joyce. Don't make any noise! We must go back to our shelves. It's time for the shop to open."

15

Roy whispered to Coy, "I'm glad you're my new friend."

Coy whispered back, "So am I, partner!"

Roy smiled. He was going to like Toy Joy.